Adult

North Yorkshire County Council Library Service

Robin Dalton was born Robin Eakin
in 1920 in Sydney. In 1946 she moved
to London, where she still lives.
Robin wrote *My Relations* in 1929
when she was eight years old.

My Relations

by Robin Ann Eakin
AGED 8, 1929

Robin Dalton

TEXT PUBLISHING MELBOURNE AUSTRALIA

Book-plate   of   Dora Solomon

"My Relations"

(fiction.)

1929

with Illustrations (coloured)

By

Robin Ann Eakin.

Dedicated to

DORA SOLOMON.

Chapter 1

It is a true saying: 'Heaven protect us from our relations.' We may choose our friends but not our relations, because they are not chosen by us. I, myself, have a plentiful supply of relatives, perhaps too plentiful! Of all relations, I think aunts are most terrifying, especially the single ones.

I have an aunt whose single-blessedness has soured her to the world. Aunt Alenia, like many other unmarried ladies, is always

Aunt Alenia Wood

trying to bring up her sister's children. Unfortunately I am an only child, so she may lavish all her care and affections upon me. I am sure Aunt Alenia must have been a model of good behaviour in her childhood. I always dread her visits, for no matter how well I behave she always finds fault with me. She means well, I am sure, but she doesn't mean much. She is a dear, good lady, but I often wish she had some children of her own.

Not all aunts are like Aunt Alenia. Auntie

Jess, for instance, is entirely different, both in appearance and in nature. She is a round, red, fussy, indulgent person, with the kindest heart in the world. Knitting seems her only occupation; she has knitted me several pairs of bed-socks, which I never wear. She is really Mummie's aunt, and is one of those old-fashioned souls who never say an unkind word. I don't think Aunt Jess could hurt a fly; it would be well if there were more of her in the world.

Auntie Jess

Chapter II

*A*unt Alenia and Aunt Jess, of whom I spoke in the last chapter, have never liked each other since the day Aunt Alenia made a fool of Uncle Ebenezer in front of everyone. Uncle Ebenezer is Auntie Jess's husband. He is, perhaps, my favourite uncle. He adores children; that is partly why I adore him. A fat kindly, old gentleman with an endless supply of jokes and funny stories. He often takes me on his knee and

'He often takes me on his knee...'

tells me the funniest stories, one after the other. He has a lovely fringe of side-whiskers and his head is perfectly bald on top. His after-dinner nap is of great importance to him, he never misses it. He and Aunt Jess are a loveable old pair. They are always ready to help others.

I will always remember an incident at a dance one night. Aunt Alenia was sitting on the balcony when a large 'romantic' looking figure in a black cloak and a false nose asked her for a dance. Aunt Alenia never dances, but she was so pleased at being asked that she consented. The black-robed figure took her into the ballroom and commenced to waltz. He told her she danced divinely and Aunt Alenia came straight home and related her adventures to us. As she was in the middle of telling how a young man had taken a fancy to her, in strode the black-robed figure. He took off the cloak and false nose and there stood Uncle Ebenezer!

It has been a great joke in the family ever since and Aunt Alenia will never hear the end of her 'black-robed figure'.

'The black-robed figure...'

Chapter III

I suppose you wonder why I have spoken of my aunts and uncles before my parents, who are really my nearest relations. True, I have a mother, who is my friend as well as my mother, though my father died three years ago. My parents, or parent, are as any other parents and I do not include them in my list of relations. Sisters and brothers, I have none, though I had a sister, Elizabeth, who died when we were both in our infancy. I do not mention half my relations in this book, as I have so many. I believe we have in our family an artist, a linguist, an actor, a plantation-owner, who is in India, and even a lunatic. This lunatic calls himself Mr Butters, and is quite mad. He writes long poems, and sends them to everyone he knows. He has written a poem about a bridge and he ends, 'The Bridge that leadeth Man to God.' However I must now tell you about my cousins, as I have more than I have aunts.

Chapter IV

*C*ousins, speaking in general, are a
hindrance rather than a pleasure. My
cousins are a queerly assorted lot and cur-
iously enough are all older than myself.
Some of them are almost old enough to be
my aunts or uncles. Of all my cousins I think
I prefer Cousin Peg. She is only three years
my senior and is a jolly, mischievous girl,
who can be cheeky without actually being
rude. She is the despair of her teachers and

Cousin Peg

considers anything a bit 'goody-goody' quite
below her. She is Aunt Kath's daughter and
is like her mother in appearance but nothing else. Perhaps I should give a description
of her before I tell you anything else. She is
tall and fairly thin, with a turned-up nose
and a much freckled face. A mop of curly
black hair frames her impudent little face
and a pair of humorous grey eyes look out
at you from under the low forehead. She
is certainly not pretty but her face has a

charm of its own that attracts you to her. I will tell you a little incident that shows you how naughty she can be.

She and I go to the same school but she is in a higher form. The headmistress, Miss Lester, or 'The Acid Drop' as we call her, was down teaching the Sixth Form Girls while the rest of the school was at play. Just outside Miss Lester's study where it can be easily seen from the top of the stairs is a bust of Shakespeare. Peg was coming up-stairs to return a book to Miss Maddocks, the botany mistress, when this bust caught her eye. Scenting mischief, she tiptoed forward and entered Miss Lester's study. Hanging on the wall opposite to the door was a peg on which was hanging a cap and gown. Peg went and got this down and took it outside. She put the gown around

Shakespeare's shoulders and placed the cap at an angle on his head. At that moment she heard footsteps and looking round saw Miss Lester standing just behind her. What happened then is too long to put in this book but it has not yet quenched Peg's spirits. I have spent a whole chapter talking about Peg. However I think we will give cousins a rest for a bit and deal with the 'young' aunts.

'Saw Miss Lester...'

Chapter V

The 'younger' aunts are a much more interesting lot. First of all I will tell you about Aunt Kath. She is, as I have mentioned before, Cousin Peg's mother, although I never knew a mother and daughter so unalike in nature. She looks like Peg's sister rather than her mother and has the same hair, eyes and nose, but her expression is shy and timid and there is nothing about her that looks impudent. Nobody in the

Auntie Kath

family takes too much notice of Aunt Kath and nobody regards her as an aunt, let alone a mother. She is very weak and shy and is glad to have a strong hand to support herself with in Peg, whose real name is Caroline Antonia Wood. I don't see where they get Peg from out of that.

Aunt Madge, Dad's youngest sister, is my favourite 'young' aunt. She is a pretty, sweet,

Aunt Madge & Uncle Ferd

Madge Wood, age four

little thing who has not yet been married a year. Uncle Ferdinand, her husband, is a little square man with a dark complexion and silent manner. I really don't see what Auntie Madge can see in him. Their ages are very different as Aunt Madge is only twenty-three and Uncle Ferdinand is thirty-seven. I have a picture of Aunt Madge when she was four. It is very funny and is very unlike her now. All this chapter is about Aunt Kath and Aunt Madge. In the next chapter we will talk about cousins again.

Chapter VI

Cousin Peg, Cousin Rosamund, and Cousin Grace are the only other 'interesting' cousins I possess. Cousin Peg, we know about, but Rosamund and Grace are still unknown. Let us deal with Rosamund first.

Cousin Rosamund is Aunt Alenia's niece and resembles Aunt Kath in a way. Her mother and father are both dead and she is brought up with Peg. Aunt Kath and she are

Cousin Rosamund

both weak and timid and both are inclined to fall back on Peg. Rosamund is a very pretty, fair little thing, with curly fair hair and big innocent blue eyes. She is always in tears and I sometimes feel like her mother in spite of her seventeen years.

Cousin Grace is the exact opposite of Cousin Rosamund and is five years her senior. A fine, strong, handsome woman with a proud haughty air. Her appearance is different to anyone in the family and she is a person to be respected. She is a quiet girl but she does not talk to me. She considers me too young. Peg, she scorns and talks of her as 'that unruly girl'. She likes Rosamund but treats her a if she were a baby. I regard her with a certain awe and I think there are times when my mother does too.

Cousin Grace

Chapter VII

I forgot to tell you in the last chapter that Rosamund is a dancer. She dances beautifully and has a lovely supply of dancing frocks. She has one dress that I love, with a little tight satin bodice and a filmy skirt of pale pink tuelle. The whole dress is

'Rosamund, a dancer.'

'Pink satin dress...'

covered with stars and there is a wand with a star on the end to hold. Rosamund does not like this dress; her favourite is a little pink satin dress she wore just recently.

We have two dancers in our family. One, Rosamund, the other a second cousin of Aunt Kath's. I have only seen her once and her name is Mavis Clandice. She is not a bit pretty and is really rather fat. Her hair is a dark reddish-brown colour, which is un-fortunate for she cannot wear pink on the stage. I suppose they called Peg after her for her second name is Caroline. Well, well, we have finished about dancers. Let us go on to artists.

Mavis Clandice

Chapter VIII

*M*y second cousin, Penelope Wood, is an artist, or at least hopes to be one. She is only sixteen but she has done some beautiful little paintings. I have one hanging in my room now. It is a landscape and is one she did when only twelve years old. She is going to her arts exam this year and two of her paintings are in the Academy. She looks like an artist, because of her dreamy expression and big brown eyes. She is Aunt

'It is a landscape…'

Madge's young sister and is very different to her. I ought to have mentioned that Aunt Madge is really my second cousin but I call her 'Aunt'. Penelope is not the only artist in the family. On one of my visits to Aunt Jessie I decided to explore the house (it's an enormous one, nearly a hundred rooms). In one of the rooms I saw the life-size picture of a beautiful

Penelope Wood

laughing babe. When I saw Auntie Jess I asked her who it was. She told me it was my own mother and the artist was my great-grandfather. I have never seen any other of his paintings but I have been told that he was a great painter.

'Picture of a laughing babe…'

Chapter IX

I have not told you yet about Uncle Jonathon. He is Aunt Alenia's brother and never were brother and sister more alike in nature. Uncle Jonathon and Uncle Ebenezer are in business together but I think Uncle Jonathon does most of the work as Uncle Ebenezer is not a business man. Uncle Jonathon is a tall, thin, loose man with a long face and greying hair. He is Irish or, at least, his mother was, though

Uncle Jonathon

'As a child...'

he speaks with a slightly Irish accent. There's a picture in Aunt Alenia's room, of Uncle Jonathon as a child. I wish I had one of Aunt Alenia too.

Speaking of pictures, in our big hall all along the side of one wall are pictures of relations dating back as far as the late seventeenth century. There is one picture, especially, that resembles Cousin Rosamund. I think it is her great-grandmother.

It is the picture of a girl looking into a mirror with her hair done in little curls on the top of the head. There is

'Her great-grannie…'

a picture of Rosamund on the other side of the wall when she was nine and they are very much alike. There is one picture there that I am sure must be some relation to Peg or Aunt Kath. It is the picture of a woman, with the same hair, eyes, nose, and expression as Peg. Nobody seems to know who she is, and I am determined to find out.

Rosamund, age nine

'Relation to Peg…'

27

Chapter X

Now I have told you in full about some of my relations I feel there are still such a lot of them unknown to you. I am going to give you a list of them with an illustration to give you some idea of what they are like. I dare say a list will be very dull but it would take more than half this book to tell all about them. We will start with Mr Butters.

I don't really know what relation I am to

Mr Butters. I think he is a second cousin of my father's. As I told you before he is a lunatic and writes or tries to write long poems. These poems he sends to everyone he knows, and sometimes he goes round on his bicycle dropping them inside garden gates. His appearance is very comical and he always wears a top-hat. His bicycle is an old-fashioned down-at-heel object that matches well with his baggy, gay-coloured trousers.

'Butters, lunatic...'

Uncle Clive

Do not be surprised if I go from Mr Butters to someone else, you must remember this is only a list.

I told you that we have in our family, a plantation-owner from India. He is Mother's step-brother and I love him. He is tall and brown with dark golden hair and deep blue eyes. His hair was naturally a very light brown but it is bleached by the sun. He comes over to England every three years and he brings with him many exciting tales of the jungle and his adventures on the plantation. His name is Clive Morris and he is forty-five.

The linguist is a very studious manly-looking woman with a plain taste and plainer appearance. She is small with a high forehead and a large pair of horn-rimmed spectacles. I have only been to her home once and it is like herself, plain and studious-looking. She is James Wood's (Aunt Jess's son) wife and is really not my blood-relation.

Now I have finished the list. In a previous chapter I mentioned that we had in our family: an artist, Penelope Wood; an actress, Mavis Clandice; a plantation owner, Clive Morris; a lunatic, Mr Butters; and the linguist, whom I have just told you about.

The linguist

Chapter XI

I have decided to tell you about my mother and father.

My mother is small, thin and rather frail-looking. She has very pale gold hair, almost white, and grey eyes. She is the same height as Penelope Wood and is rather like Rosamund in nature, though not so timid. My father, I barely remember, but I know he was older than my mother. From what I can remember he was medium height

My Mother

My Father

with brown hair and black eyes. He was very slight but wiry and he was as brown as a berry. He was a handsome man but he looked more like a young boy. His Christian name he never used as it was a burden to any man. Wattle, or Wat for short. He changed it to Walter and only his own family knew his real name.

You may think it queer, but now I have told you about my parents, I am going to tell you about myself. Of course, I cannot tell you about my own nature, but I can at least give you my appearance. I am supposed to be like my father and, indeed, I have the same black eyes, the same small figure, and the same small, snub nose. My hair is really a kind of ruddy brown, perhaps more red than brown, and it reaches down past my shoulders. I am fourteen and considered very small for my age. This is a tiny chapter but I have so many interesting things to tell you in the next one that it will make up for it. Let us go on to the Blossoms.

Myself

Chapter XII

*E*nter the Blossom family. They are or their mother is a second cousin of Dad's. There are seven adorable little Blossoms and a mother Blossom; the father is dead. First we will deal with the mother of them all, Beery Blossom.

With a name like that any woman ought to go mad, but not so Mrs Blossom. She is a fat, kindly lazy old soul who is as uneducated as she is lazy. She has a passion for anything

Beery Blossom   *Bob Blossom*

romantic and has never done a scrap of
work in her life. Her children keep the
house, or at least her second-eldest daughter
does, while she sits and watches dreamily
not thinking for a moment that she is at
all lazy. Being romantic, she has given her
children the most terrible names, all of
which are names of flowers. I think Blossom
is bad enough without a worse Christian
name. The only two in the family who are
not burdened by them are the two eldest
boys who were named by their father. We
will go in ages, taking Bob Blossom first.

Bob Blossom is nineteen, a clever, quiet, shy boy with a lot of brains but a proud air that forbids him to accept a favour from anybody. He seldom speaks, and nobody counts him as head of the family and he is too wrapped up in his work to assert himself. He is tall and fair with grey eyes and a quiet manner. After Bob, comes Billy Blossom, that reckless, irresistible scamp of fourteen years. Billy's importance is a thing to be respected among the Blossoms. He is head of the family and is the mischief and despair of the neighbourhood. Billy is a very small, square boy with a shock of red hair and a plentiful supply of freckles. I have not yet met anyone who did not love Billy Blossom.

Billy

Pan Blossom

May Blossom

The next on the list is Pansy Blossom or Pan. She is a brilliant, lovable child with the mind of someone twice her age. She, though only thirteen, is a promising author with a passion for books. She is writing a book on socialism and has not time to help with the housework as she is always learning or writing. She is very dark and thin with big brown eyes and a tangled mass of black hair. May Blossom, age ten, is the little housewife. A plump, pretty, kind little girl with fair hair and blue eyes. She is clever with her needle and the Blossoms owe all their clothes to her skilful fingers. It is she who cooks their meals and does the housework; she strives to keep their little home neat and clean,

Wat Blossom

while the mother of them all gossips to her friends. Poor May, she gets little thanks and, indeed, she is the most worthy of them.

The fifth of the Blossom children was called after my father Wattle Blossom. Poor Wat is a second edition of Billy, a little quieter and not so sure of himself. He is a dear little boy and helps May to the best of his ability with the work. He is only seven and is like Bob in appearance. He is perhaps a little fatter but otherwise they are very alike.

Peach Blossom, the most adorable peach

Peach Blossom

'The Oldest Baby...'

ever seen, is only five. She is exactly like you would imagine an angel with hair like silk and a complexion like peaches and cream. She is called 'Peachie' and has the most loveable and sympathetic nature in the world. She is a beauty-worshipper; her little face lights up when she sees anything beautiful. She and Billy are the greatest of friends and he often confides in this faithful little soul his most intimate secrets.

The baby of the family, Buds Blossom, is nicknamed the Oldest Baby. It is a fitting name for the poor little three-year-old. She is small and weary looking with an old, old, wise wizened-up face. It is sad to look at her for she has so little spirit. The only one in the family who can rouse any spirit in her is Wat, and he admits it is hard. She is not like anyone in the family but she has hair just like Pan's.

This has been a long chapter but I hope you have enjoyed hearing about Beery Blossom and all the little Blossoms.

Chapter XIII

I suppose you must think that I have quite exhausted my supply of relations, but I have not. I am going to tell you about Cousin Gwen.

How I really got to know Cousin Gwen was through Aunt Madge. Cousin Gwen is her step-sister, and Gwennie and I are great friends.

Every time Aunt Madge came to see Mummie she praised Gwen all through her visit, telling how clever and pretty she was and what beautiful golden curls she had. In fact, I was so sick of hearing of this unknown Gwen that I felt I hated her. Aunt Madge was always talking of her beautiful little hands, her well-cut clothes, her polite manner, and above all how good she was. I put up with this until one day my mother received a letter saying that Cousin Gwen was coming to stay with us. Aunt Madge came to see us the day before she arrived and there was an unusual twinkle in her eye. However, when the time came for Gwennie to arrive I went down the path feeling irreproachably clean, with my new silk frock on. A big blue car was stopping at the gate and a chauffeur in a plum-coloured uniform got out and opened the door.

Out stepped Cousin Gwen in a faultless

Cousin Gwen

coat and hat with the famous curls over her
shoulders. She put out a tiny, slender, gloved
hand and smiled the most brilliant smile. I
put back my shoulders and took her inside.
Then followed the most hectic three weeks
when I was on my very best behaviour. I
had to admit that all Aunt Madge had said
about Gwennie was true. On the last day of
her visit we were left alone in the house, or
at least in the garden. As Mummie left, she
told us not to put our heads through the

bars in the gate. I don't know why she did, I thought it rather a silly thing to say. As soon as she was out of sight Gwen turned on me. 'Oh I'm so sick of you, you're always so good. I'm sick of being on my best behaviour, I'm going to put my head through the bars.'

Too surprised to say anything, I watched her wriggle her head through. She looked up at me. 'There,' she said, 'you needn't look so shocked,' and so saying she tried to take her head out, but it wouldn't come.

'She couldn't do it…'

I don't really know what happened then except that after ten minutes wriggling I went for the joiner who lives next door. The bars were soon cut through and Gwennie was standing shaking out her rumpled curls.

'Well,' she said, when we were both inside, 'now you know I'm not a bit good. I just thought I'd show Madge how good I could be. I was sick of hearing how clever, how pretty, how good you were.'

Then the whole story came out bit by bit, and Aunt Madge was very unpopular just then. Gwennie had to go but she has been lots of times since, and she and I are the greatest of friends.

Chapter XIV

*G*wen took up a whole chapter and now I am going to tell you about Kitty.

Kitty Moreton is my father's step-sister's child and a kind of step-cousin. She has more or less the same nature as Peg but is very daring and much naughtier than Peg. I had not met her until about five months ago but I had heard a lot about her.

The night of our annual fancy-dress dance I had to go to bed early because everyone in the house was going to the dance. It has always been my grievance that I am not allowed to go to the dance, but my mother is very firm on that point.

Well, on this particular evening I was feeling very cross. If I had not I probably would not have done what I did. About nine o'clock I heard a sound behind me and looking round I saw a shadowy figure in the doorway. I asked who it was and the figure replied, 'I'm Kitty Moreton, I do think it's stiff you not being allowed to go to the dance so I've come to take you.'

I gasped in surprise and got into the old-fashioned frock Kitty had brought me as well as I could in the dark. Not waiting to put on a coat, I took the hand of the unknown Kitty and together we raced downstairs, into the garden, and on to the ballroom.

Kitty Moreton

As soon as we reached the brilliantly lit room I turned round and looked at my companion. She was a tall, pretty, dark girl with a cheerful smile and twinkly brown eyes. She looked about sixteen and was dressed as a kind of columbine in pale green and gold. I put myself in her hands and she certainly looked after me well. I avoided anyone I knew and I looked quite different in my dress. When supper was over Kitty whispered that I had better go,

'In my dress…'

and told me to give the dress to an old woman who would call in the morning. I thanked her and ran home, wondering a little at her words. In the morning at about ten o'clock there was a knock at the door. My mother answered it and went to get some old clothes. Wondering at her action I went to the door to see who it was.

It was an old, dirty woman with a big basket over her arm. When I came out she

looked up at me and a pair of brown eyes
smiled at me. Guessing who it was, I ran
upstairs, got the dress and gave it to her. She
stuffed it into her basket and shuffled away.
My mother came down with a big bundle
and finding she had gone was angry. That is
how I first met Kitty.

'She looked at me…'

Chapter XV

When I mentioned that all my cousins were older than myself I made a mistake. I had forgotten Amelia Jane, Mavis Clandice's daughter. Amelia Jane is a very independent young woman of five years and three months. She has a very exaggerated idea of her own importance and is the cheekiest, funniest little person I have ever met. Her mother has allowed her to do what she likes, and her idea of her own

Amelia Jane

importance first began when she dismissed her own nurse at three years old. She has shortened her Christian name 'Amelia Jane' to 'Meely' and nothing can induce her to change it. Meely is really rather an ugly child except for her beautiful hair that somewhat resembles her mother's. She is very tall for her age and thin and awkward-looking. She has a little snub nose, a big mouth and bright little dark eyes. Meely is a great friend of Peachie's, and Peachie regards her as a little queen. Meely is rather selfish without knowing it. In the little child-games they play, Meely always is the Queen or Princess or whatever the case may be. Her independence overawes Peachie who is quite content to be the servant.

One day I went into Meely's room and saw Meely in her mother's dress with a crown on her head, sitting on the table ordering Peachie about. Peachie was dressed in a very old dress of mine that I use as an overall

Peach Blossom

when I am helping with the housework. Meely seemed to think that she was being very unselfish and Peachie was content to be her servant.

*

Now we must say goodbye to my relations. I have finished the list and I hope you have enjoyed reading it. I am going to draw all the people in this book so that you may see them together.

My Relations

 Aunt Alenia

 Mavis Clandice

 Aunt Jessie

 Penelope Wood

 Uncle Ebenezer

 Uncle Jonathon

 Cousin Peg

 Mr Butters

 Auntie Kath

 Uncle Clive

 Auntie Madge

 Mrs Wood

 Uncle Ferdinand

 Mother

 Cousin Rosamund

 My Father

 Cousin Grace

 Myself